OVERFLOW

a student's guide to giving

scotty gibbons

Overflow
A Student's Guide to Giving
By Scotty Gibbons

Printed in the United States of America
ISBN: 1-880689-24-3
Copyright 2009, Scotty Gibbons and Onward Books, Inc.

Cover design by Scott Wiskus, Grand & Weller, grandandweller.com
Back cover photo by James Pauls, Eyecrave, eyecrave.com

Unless otherwise indicated, all Scripture references are from the
Holy Bible: New International Version, copyright 1984, Zondervan
Bible Publishers. Scripture quotations marked *NLT* are taken from
the *New Living Translation*, copyright 1996, 2004, Tyndale House
Publishers. Scripture quotations marked *The Message* are taken from
The Message: The New Testament, Psalms and Proverbs, copyright
1993, 1994, 1995, NavPress Publishing Group.

dedication

To the students and leaders of Realife, who model through their giving and their living, lives of true overflow.

"This service that you perform is not only supplying the needs of God's people but is also overflowing in many expressions of thanks to God" (2 Corinthians 9:12).

contents

overflow

"I'm going to have to call you back ..."

I cut the conversation short, tossed my phone on the coffee table, and walked quickly toward the kitchen.

Before I was halfway there, I saw it sliding across the floor, silently and slowly. It inched around the corner as if to welcome me into the room. I stepped carefully into the kitchen and immediately realized that the problem was even larger than I had first thought! In fact, it was growing by the second. Who knows, if I hadn't escaped out the back door to the safety of the deck, I may have been overwhelmed by an unfamiliar white force that was threatening to take over the entire house!

"Scott, what in the world did you do in there?" I interrupted my roommate who was relaxing on the deck with a book.

"Do what?" he looked up from his reading.

"That's what!" I said, pointing at the sliding door to the kitchen. The view through the glass was like the inside of one of those huge washing machines at the Laundromat, suds crawling up the door.

"Oh, shoot!" Scott dropped his book, jumped to his feet, and charged into an overflowing ocean of white foam and bubbles.

Running at first—then slipping and sliding—Scott made his way to the source of the substance: the dishwasher. "I don't know what happened! The dishwasher was full, so I just turned it on."

"What did you put in there?" I laughed. "Liquid bubbles?"

Fumbling for the on/off switch through the suds, Scott started to explain. "I just used dishwashing soap!"

"Did you use the detergent made for the dishwasher, or the concentrated stuff that you use to wash dishes by hand?"

"Aren't they the same thing?" Scott looked up and across the room, assessing the damages.

I smiled, "Apparently not!"

What is overflow?

Did you know that God's perfect plan is that you would live a life that overflows? I'm not talking about some kind of accidental mess (a la my dishwasher). I'm talking about living a life of purpose that overflows to bless those around you.

God wants to fill your life so abundantly full that His goodness and glory spill out and point others to Him!

Jesus said that his followers would have streams of living water flow from within them (John 7:38). He was painting a picture to communicate what a life completely dedicated to God looks like. Water is one of the most powerful forces on earth. Life with God is like a stream of living water—refreshing, life-giving, and powerful.

When you come to Jesus, you let go of your old life—the one that was heading nowhere, dead and dry—so that God can give you a whole new life. And since He doesn't do anything halfway, you don't just get a sip of living water. God immerses you in new life! He wants to fill you full to overflowing so that everywhere you go, you splash living water.

I like how the apostle Paul captures the idea of overflow: "God is able to make all grace abound to you, so that in all things at all times, having all that you need, you will abound in every good work" (2 Corinthians 9:8). Even the language in this verse overflows! Did you notice all of the *alls*, the *abounds* and the *every*? God is able to make *all* grace abound to you so that you have *all* that you need in *all* things and at *all* times. You know what *all* and *every* mean; Paul is talking about the whole enchilada—God is able to help you in every way! In case you're less clear on the word *abound*, it means to exist in large amounts. Why does God want to bless us so abundantly? It's because He wants us to abound in every good work. How incredible!

Take a minute and think about all of the different ways your life could overflow—through an encouraging word spoken at just the right time, through the good example set for the friend that needs it, through the love shown to those who might not return the favor. There are all kinds of ways that God can work through you to bless others! The possibilities are endless, but the result is predictable.

Check out what Paul says will happen: "This service that you perform is not only supplying the needs of God's people but is also overflowing in many expressions of thanks to God" (2 Corinthians 9:12).

When you open your life up to overflow, you are blessed, others are blessed, and God gets all of the credit!

One of the most practical ways you can see overflow work in your life is through giving. Why? Finances is the one area where God invites us to test him "and see if [He] will not throw open the floodgates of heaven and pour out so much blessing that [we] will not have room enough for it" (Malachi 3:10). Jesus said something similar: "Give, and it will be given to you. A good measure, pressed down, shaken together and running over, will be poured into your lap" (Luke 6:38). That sounds like overflow to me!

Overflow at Realife

This book is a result of what can only be described as an "overflow explosion" at our church, James River Assembly (where I'm privileged to be the youth pastor of more than 1,000 incredible teenagers). What we experienced over the course of 11 weeks in the southwestern corner of the Show-Me State (aka Missouri) is nothing short of astounding! Week after week, I was overwhelmed by how powerfully God worked in the lives of our students and volunteer leaders. He did more than we ever imagined possible, specifically in this area of giving.

As a student ministry, we set an aggressive goal: raise $50,000 for missions in less than three months! When I heard how much the students pledged to give that first night of our missions project, I gulped ... hard. I was one-part stoked and one-part freaked out of my mind. As a youth pastor, I always encourage our students to trust God to do something huge (apparently, they got the message). But as a leader—and I hate to admit this—there was a part of me that was concerned that our goal might not be realistic. I tried to imagine what our end of the year celebration service might look like if we fell short: "Alrighty! Well ... we didn't exactly hit our goal. In fact, we missed it by a long shot. Bummer! But hey, next year at Realife is going to be awesome, so invite your friends!"

Any nervousness I had about not hitting our goal dissolved almost immediately. After all, I believe in the importance of giving generously to missions. Ralph Harris put it this way: "One well equipped missionary can do the job of 10 under-equipped missionaries." Beyond that, I sensed in my heart that God was doing something unique with this project—I couldn't wait to see what it was! After the first few weeks of the project, it was crystal clear to me that God was helping us. I was amazed to see God's favor poured out on our group and the fervor it produced in us to pursue our goal. I was literally overwhelmed by the stories I heard throughout the project! It seems like one minute I'd get an email from a student who did something so sacrificial it made me want to cry. And the next, I'd hear about a group of students that came up with some hilarious idea to raise money for missions that made me laugh out loud (that's LOL, for those of you who prefer the abbreviation). I'm so excited to share many of these Realife stories with you in the following pages as we look at the principles that will help you to live an overflowing life! Unfortunately, there's not enough room in this book for every story, but to whet your appetite for those you will read, check out some of these highlights:

Matt, a college student, planned to give plasma as part of a big plan he and his wife came up with for raising money. He earned $40 from that little effort and he definitely earned it. It turns out that the nurse didn't puncture his vein correctly, his arm filled up with blood, and he ended up passing out! Yikes! There's got to be a better way to help missionaries!

Bekah, a junior high student, got her friends together and made all kinds of stuff out of colored duct tape—stuff like purses and wallets. With a lot of hard work (and a lot of duct tape), Bekah earned $370 and gave it all to missions!

Kaitlyn, a high school student, emailed me to ask how exactly she should go about giving nearly $50 in change in the offering. She and her family had collected the change over the course of the drive, but Kaitlyn was a little nervous about overloading the offering bucket. It was really heavy and she didn't know if Realife's offering-taker-uppers had the brute strength required to collect her coin. I encouraged her to go to the bank and exchange it for small, unmarked bills with consecutive serial numbers instead. OK, maybe I wasn't that specific ...

Olivia, a junior high student whose parents have a photography studio downtown, asked her neighbors to donate baked goods for missions. Then, she sold these delectable delights at her parents' photography studio during a popular monthly arts event called *First Friday Artwalk*. In just a few hours, she raised $80 for missions!

Christopher, a junior high student, worked really hard doing extra chores and odd jobs to meet his $120 giving goal. After he had already met his goal, Christopher heard about a contest at Realife: the fastest student to solve a Rubik's cube puzzle would win an iPod. Christopher practiced every day until the contest, won the iPod, sold it, and gave the proceeds to missions—he exceeded his giving goal by $1 !

John and Bev, leaders at Realife, mobilized the team of students and volunteers that they lead to hold what they called a "quote-a-thon." Their team regularly memorizes entire books of the Bible, so they found sponsors willing to support missions by paying to hear these Scriptures quoted. Several hours and hundreds of verses later, the Realife Quiz Team collected $2,020.97! What's even cooler is that John and Bev are taking this concept to the national level and getting other groups to raise money for missions, too. Talk about overflow! I can't wait to see what happens across the country as a result of this team's creativity and commitment to missions!

By the time all was said and done, God helped Realife give $75,389 to missions in less than three months!

As if exceeding our goal by 50% wasn't remarkable enough, what really amazed me is how we experienced this overflow in a really tough time, financially speaking. At the time of the drive, America had just been plunged to the depths of an economic recession and our church was in the middle of a major building project (which many of our students were already supporting financially). Even though the odds were stacked against us, what we were able to accomplish with God's help is now overflowing to bless missionaries around the world!

You can experience overflow in your own life—and you won't even have to go near the dishwasher!

In the following pages, I'll be sharing principles that will help you experience overflow firsthand through the joy of a generous life. You're going to read true stories of students just like you— stories of sacrifice, of great faith, of miraculous provision, and much more. What ties them all together is overflow—God working so powerfully in the life of an individual that the effects are literally felt around the world.

Did You Know ...

Teens' discretionary income increases from nearly $1,500 at age 12 and 13 to nearly $4,500 by age 16 and 17!

(*Teen Market Profile 2004*, Magazine Publishers of America)

application questions

1. What is one practical step that you can take to share your overflowing life with others?

2. What are some ways that your life can overflow to reach the lost at school or work?

3. What are some concerns that you have about setting a giving goal that would stretch your faith? What about it is exciting to you?

4. If you could write a story about your youth ministry's missions giving this year, what would you want it to be?

5. How can you help make that story become a reality?

2

abundance

When someone has been given much,
much will be required in return.
Luke 12:48 (*NLT*)

Do you consider yourself "rich"? Most teenagers don't. But think about this for just a second. A person who earns $25,000 a year—not exactly someone we'd consider to be "loaded" by American standards—actually earns more than almost 90% of the world's population! That's unbelievable! That means that if you have an average entry-level job in America, you are actually in the top 10% of the world's wealthy. Cha-cha-cha-ching!

Even more shocking: someone earning a middle-class American income of $50,000 a year is better off than 99% of the world's population!

That's right, a middle class American bringing home $50K is in the top 1% of the world's wealthy. Wow! That provides quite a perspective, doesn't it?

As a nation, we are obsessed with the lifestyles of the rich and famous. From the TV to the Internet to the supermarket tabloids, we see a continual parade of pop culture prosperity. In fact, we see wealth so much in America, we are somehow fooled into thinking that we're poor because we don't have as much as this celebrity or sports star. That's crazy! Just because we don't have the money to buy that new game system the instant it hits the market … just because we can't afford to buy that fifth pair of jeans until our next payday … just because we drive a car that rolled off the line before Y2K, doesn't make us poor.

The opposite is actually true—we literally live in the lap of luxury in America! You may not think of yourself as rich, but by every global standard, you are. You may as well be rolling in it! The fact that you're reading this book right now, not concerned with where your next meal is going to come from or where you're going to sleep tonight is an indicator of how blessed you really are. We live in huge, climate-controlled homes with a bedroom for everyone. We drive nice cars; in fact most families own more than one. We enjoy clean drinking water (effortlessly from the tap). We eat great food—if we don't have any at home, we can literally drive up to a window in the side of a building and get food in a bag so that we can feed our faces without leaving the comfort of our cars!

I don't bring American abundance to your attention to make you feel guilty; after all, I'm just as blessed (and am very thankful that I am). I'm pointing it out because it gives us a great perspective on the verse that opened this chapter. Jesus said that "when someone has been given much, much will be required in return" (Luke 12:48, *NLT*). Few people on the planet will be held to a higher standard than you or I. We've been given so much that God expects much in return.

I don't know about you, but the realization that we are so abundantly blessed makes me want to live a lifestyle of generous overflow! I have more than I need. In return, I want to be a giver! After all, many of the things you and I take for granted—food, clean water, shelter, and healthcare—are matters of life and death in less fortunate countries around the world.

Take Mike and Laura Clark's story as an example. Mike and Laura are good friends of mine. As volunteers, they used to oversee Realife's college ministry. An incredible couple who have literally put their own lives at risk to do some incredible work for God, Mike and Laura Clark have been in some 50 countries over the last few years. Their work focuses specifically on relief and development, helping the poorest of the poor and those affected by natural disasters or conflicts.

Most of Mike and Laura's time has been spent in Haiti. On one of their recent trips, they met two little kids, Mackenlove (a boy) and Michelove (his little sister). The father of these kids was nowhere to be found when their mother died from a disease she most likely contracted from drinking filthy water—a disease that she was unable to fight off in her state of malnutrition. Mackenlove and Michelove were orphaned, even though they didn't understand the concept. In fact, for more than a week, they stayed with their mom's rotting body! Occasionally, they would go out into the streets, begging and scrounging for food that they would then bring back to their mom in hopes of reviving her. As a father of four beautiful girls, my heart is absolutely broken by stories like this.

When Mackenlove and Michelove's extended family realized what had happened, they took the two kids in, but not because they wanted to help. Instead, the family made these starving little kids with no parents their slaves. Before long, they ran away, preferring the uncertainty of life on the streets to the misery of being enslaved to their relatives. About this time, Mike and Laura's team ran across the two orphans, as one team member described in their journal:

This morning I held a four year old child who was nothing more than skin and bones. Barely able to hold her head up, I heard her whisper the softest cry: "M'grangou," which means, "I'm hungry." It was at that very moment that my heart slipped—*I need to do SOMETHING* was all I could think. I handed her over to a friend, who was sitting with her brother, and ran up the hill. A few minutes later, I was back with a baggie of food. Watching them eat broke me. I've never seen children so hungry in all my life.

Within a few seconds of seeing these children, I knew the situation was serious. Their lifeless eyes and dirty, bony bodies told the sad story of hunger and neglect. We did what we could for them, providing some clothing, shoes, and food. But at the end of the day, we had to send them on their way.

Over the weeks, I have visited them a few times and have learned a little more of their story. I doubt we will ever have all the details, but their past is not nearly as important to me as their future. A future which will be filled with loving care, smiles, laughter, nutritious meals three times a day, a warm bed to sleep in, a roof over their heads, and an activities coordinator named Rachel loving on them everyday. Yes, Lord willing, these children will be in our care at the Hope House in just a few days.

I don't know about you, but I can't begin to relate to the situation that these kids found themselves in. I am so abundantly blessed. I'm thankful for missionaries like Mike and Laura who are doing such remarkable work for God in such difficult situations. And yet, I recognize that I have a responsibility, too. That's why my wife, Casey, and I support Mike and Laura financially—it's the least we can do! We've been given so much and we understand that God expects much in return.

The goal of this chapter is not to make you feel guilty. Don't feel guilty because you were born in America—do something! This chapter is simply meant to give you some perspective, to help you understand how abundantly blessed you really are. You're loaded!

God has given you so much! Instead of thinking about what you don't have; think about all that you do have.

Doesn't that make you want to do something big for someone in need? Doesn't it inspire you to dream a big dream and do a big thing for God? I know it motivates me! God hasn't blessed me just so I can enjoy it. I'm blessed to be a blessing to someone else. God has given you so much, what are you going to do with it?

In the next chapter, you're going to hear about a guy who had quite an abundant little business—if you consider $50 billion "little." Read on to find out how he blew it all!

Did You Know ...

The average American child grows up in a home with 3 televisions, 2 music players, 3 radios, 2 VCRs, 1 video game player, and 1 computer.

(University of Washington, 2003)

application questions

1. Take a moment to think about how blessed you really are. How can you use that God-given abundance to help others?

2. What steps can you take to make sure that you keep a healthy perspective about money in the midst of abundance?

3. When you receive or earn money, will you handle it any differently in light of the stories in this chapter? How?

4. How can you use your abundance to do something big for someone in need?

5. One of the ways you can give out of your abundance is by going on a missions trip. What are some other things you can do to meet needs and share the gospel?

3

stewardship

A person who is put in charge
as a manager must be faithful.
1 Corinthians 4:2 (*NLT*)

People trusted Bernard Madoff with their money. Lots of
people. And lots of money ($50 billion to be exact). Madoff
seemed to be an investing whiz who was always ahead of the
market. His clients gave him their money to invest and he
"invested" it. Everyone was happy … until the economy fell
apart. When it did, a lot of Madoff's investors wanted to
withdraw their money so they didn't lose it in the stock market.
When that happened, Madoff's $50 billion empire collapsed
like a cheap house of cards (and so did the financial futures of
the countless individuals and corporations who had trusted
him with their money)! That's a rough week at the office!

What happened? Instead of investing people's money, Madoff is accused of moving it all around. As he received investments from new clients, he allegedly turned around and gave it to existing clients (who thought it was interest that they were earning on their own money). Eventually, the money ran out and the whole scheme collapsed. People lost everything they had invested with this guy! Entire organizations have nearly collapsed because their budgets were managed by Madoff. The results were so devastating that some connected to the situation have even gone so far as to take their own life! Yet, as I'm writing this chapter, Bernard Madoff is under house arrest in his swanky $7 million luxury apartment in New York City. The poor people caught up in this huge scandal wish they were so lucky!

Can you believe that? So many people worked hard their entire lives, scrimping and saving to ensure their financial futures, only to lose it all because this guy was allegedly playing games with their cash. Just like that (I just snapped my fingers—feel free to re-read this sentence and snap your fingers for effect), everything these responsible people had worked for was gone! Snap!

Why the update on Madoff, you ask? Well, this story powerfully illustrates one of the most important principles we need to understand when it comes to overflow: *stewardship*.

Even if you don't know the dictionary definition of the word, you probably understand the concept of stewardship. Here's the idea: if someone asks you to take care of something for them, you do so responsibly. Stewardship is that simple, but apparently Bernie didn't get the memo. He was supposed to take care of—to be a good steward of—his clients' money. Why? Because the money wasn't his in the first place; he was simply asked to take care of it so that his clients could get it back with interest when they needed it.

On a lighter note (a *much* lighter note), I walked into my office the other day and there was a HUGE box of Reese's Peanut Butter Cups on my desk (we're talking about a Sam's Club special, here). That doesn't happen every day and I was curious to know where it came from, so I read the note taped to the top (brilliant, I know). The peanut butter-packed parcel was from Jonathan, a college student at Realife. Jonathan really enjoyed giving in Realife's missions project—so much so in fact, that he put it into practice and splurged on some sugary goodness to thank our staff.

As much as I appreciated Jonathan's gesture, what really impressed me was his understanding of stewardship. This wasn't Jonathan's first time to give to missions. In 2006, he sensed that God was asking him to give $1,200 to missions.

He didn't see how that was possible as a 16 year old, given that he was only making $5 a week mowing the yard. But he knew that if God had spoken to him about the amount, He was also able to provide it.

Jonathan was faithful to respond to God's leading. He immediately went out to find a job. That year, Jonathan gave a whopping 85% of his income to missions (after giving his 10% tithe, of course)! With God's help and a lot of hard work, he exceeded his goal that year, giving $1,232 to the cause of Christ above and beyond his tithe. The next year, Jonathan felt God leading him to set a goal of $3,000. He worked hard again, God opened up new job opportunities, and by the end of the year, God had helped him to give $3,502. In the last two and a half years, Jonathan has given $6,451.10 to missions!

Do you know why Jonathan was able to hit his aggressive giving goals? It's because he understands stewardship. Whether he's giving 10% of his income or 100%, Jonathan understands that every dollar he earns belongs to God. You're a steward of God's money too! God has entrusted some valuable things to your care. In 1 Corinthians 4:2, the apostle Paul says it this way: "… a person who is put in charge as a manager must be faithful." God expects us to take good care of His resources, just like Jonathan did.

Here's a crazy (but true) thought: *everything that we think of as ours really belongs to God.*

My personality came from God. Your talents came from God. Even our time isn't our own—every moment is a gift from our Creator. God is the one who's provided every dollar, every meal, every piece of clothing throughout your whole life. The house you live in belongs to God. The car you drive belongs to God. Even the nasty microwave burrito that you're munching on right now (feel free to substitute the snack item of your choice) came to you courtesy of the King of kings.

At some point, one way or another, we will give everything that we call "ours" back to God. When we do, we're going to give an account to God for the way we've used His money (much like Madoff is going to have to answer for the use of his clients' money). I'm confident that the outcome in your situation is going to be a lot more positive!

When you have time, I'd encourage you to read the Parable of the Talents found in Matthew 25:14-30. It paints an interesting picture of stewardship. In this parable, a wealthy king is going on a trip, so he entrusts some of his material wealth to three of his servants—who we'll call Larry, Moe, and

Curly. He gives Larry five talents—by the way, *talent* doesn't refer to your ability to drink milk through your nose … it's actually a measurement of money that was worth a few years' wages. Moe got three talents, and Curly got one. He distributed the money in different amounts according to his servants' different abilities.

In the story, Larry and Moe manage the king's money wisely. In fact, they put it to work in good investments and double their master's money. Curly, however, is afraid of the king. He doesn't really know what to do with his master's money and apparently doesn't care enough to try and find out, so he buries it in the backyard next to his dead dog (OK, the part about the dead dog might not be in there).

When the king returns, he asks his servants to explain how they used his money. Larry and Moe explain that they wisely stewarded the king's money, earning more for him in his absence. Because they were faithful with the little they were given, the king entrusted them with more and they were abundantly blessed. We don't know what they did with this new financial opportunity. But based on their track record, we can assume they used the king's funds wisely—perhaps to open a wildly successful investment bank in the kingdom that provided sound investing strategies for all of the king's constituents.

We do know that Curly wasn't as fortunate as his friends. Because he was lazy and mishandled the king's money, he ... well ... you can read it for yourself in Matthew 25. Let's just say he didn't get promoted to shift manager (and he didn't get house arrest in a luxury apartment). Bummer!

I don't know about you, but I want to honor God by being a good steward of His money!

The first step toward an overflowing life is an understanding that everything you "own" is actually on loan. When you stop to consider the fact that we're going to give an account to God for the way we use His money, it makes you think twice about doubling down on that $4 latte or splurging on that sixth pair of shoes. Not that there's anything wrong with enjoying coffee, or wearing shoes. But as a good steward, you are more concerned with honoring God with your money and making it count for eternity, than you are in consuming it all on the material pleasures of this world.

Think of the incredible impact that Jonathan made in just a few short years! He's a normal guy simply trying to do his best, and the result is overflow. One of the coolest things Jonathan said about his experience is how much he's enjoyed coming to a place in his life where he no longer worries about money—that's possible because he understands stewardship: it all belongs to God anyway. Another reason Jonathan doesn't have to worry about finances is because his experience has taught him something else—something we're going to learn from a guy nicknamed "Z-FUNK!" in the next chapter ...

Did You Know ...

Using the Internet to compare prices can help you save up to 55% on MP3 players, video games and CDs—even if you don't buy online!

application questions

1. Are there some areas in your life where you haven't been a good steward? What are they?

2. What can you do to become a better steward in these areas?

3. When you realize that everything you have belongs to God, how does that change the way you view or handle your possessions?

4. If you were to give an account to God today about the way you spend your money, what do you think He would say in response?

5. Have you ever developed a budget to help you become a better steward of your money? Why not start today?

4

contentment

We brought nothing into the world,
and we can take nothing out of it.
1 Timothy 6:7

Does anything about this news story seem weird to you?

> CORNWALL, Connecticut (AP)—The son of
> billionaire oil tycoon T. Boone Pickens was charged
> with burglary after he was found hiding under a table
> in a fly fishing shop, authorities said.
>
> Michael Pickens, 51, spent three days in jail following
> his arraignment Monday in Bantam Superior Court.
> He was found Sunday inside the Housatonic Meadows

Fly Shop after the store's owner noticed something wrong and called police, according to state police.

Investigators found a nearby stash of items taken from the shop and found Pickens groggy and hiding under a table inside, state police said.

Pickens, of Nocona, Texas, had rented a room nearby for a weekend of fishing ...

OK, let me get this straight, Michael ... Your dad is a billionaire (with a "b"). He's an oil tycoon. He pretty much owns the state of Texas. And you get arrested for stealing—wait for it ... wait for it—bait! You're on your way to go fishing, probably off the side of your dad's yacht, and you decide to stop by the tackle shop to steal 75 cents worth of worms! Unbelievable!

Isn't that crazy? Maybe you've heard about David Joe White Jr. After pleading guilty to 42 burglary charges, this guy was rearrested for swiping his lawyer's portable tape recorder ... from the defense table in the court room! Picture it: this guy is in court being arraigned for burglary and apparently the judge is looking away, so Junior treats himself to the ol' five-finger discount on his lawyer's tape recorder! You may be wondering who in their right mind would steal a tape recorder, and that's a great point. Even crazier is stealing one while you're in court to plead guilty for 42 counts of burglary!

To put it mildly, these two guys don't understand contentment. Simply put, contentment is being satisfied with what you have. Honestly, living with a content heart can be downright difficult! Because our society relentlessly pursues more and more stuff, we're constantly being bombarded by messages that work against contentment. We are literally marketed to from every side. Think about it. From mass media TV ads to search-specific Google ads to friendly (or not so friendly) Facebook ads to cell phone and email spam, we are constantly being told by this world that what we have isn't enough: We need more! We need bigger! We need better! We need brighter! We need faster! And most of all—we need it NOW!

So, why is contentment important? For one thing, contentment is the key to an enjoyable life.

When you're living in a place of contentment, you can experience overflowing joy that doesn't depend on life's circumstances. If you're not content, you're going to be miserable every time life gets hard. For example, contentment is the reason that the apostle Paul was able to write the book of Philippians while he was suffering in the bottom of a dirty dungeon. Do you know what's really remarkable about that? Biblical scholars often refer to the book of Philippians—the book Paul wrote while chained to a wall in unthinkable conditions—as "the epistle of joy"! Out of all of Paul's writings, the one where Paul is the most joyful is the one where he finds himself in the worst possible situation. Now that's an overflowing life!

Check out what Paul says about contentment in chapter 4 (remember he's writing from a small, stinking rat-hole of a room where he's not exactly receiving 5-star service): "Actually, I don't have a sense of needing anything personally. I've learned by now to be quite content whatever my circumstances. I'm just as happy with little as with much, with much as with little. I've found the recipe for being happy whether full or hungry, hands full or hands empty. Whatever I have, wherever I am, I can make it through anything in the One who makes me who I am" (Philippians 4:10b-13, *The Message*).

Paul's contentment is amazing! Don't you want that kind of joy? I know I do. In fact, you can sign me up for two of whatever he's got (minus the chains and the dirty dungeon)!

Another reason contentment is important is because it helps us keep our priorities straight.

Contentment breaks the power of materialism in our life so that we can experience overflow.

It reminds us that life isn't about stuff, which frees us up to live a life of generosity. Writing to his son in the faith, Paul reminded Timothy that "we brought nothing into the world, and we can take nothing out of it" (1 Timothy 6:7).

So how did Paul come to this place of contentment? The key is found in the last verse of the passage we read earlier. In *The Message*, Paul says, "I can make it through anything in the One who makes me who I am" (Philippians 4:13). I like how straightforward the *NIV* translates it: "I can do everything through him who gives me strength." The power to live a life of contentment, a life overflowing, comes from God! You and I are powerless to live a life of contentment on our own. But we can do everything through Christ, who offers us His strength. How incredible!

At the beginning of our missions project, Angela felt like God wanted her to set a goal of $400. As a college student without much money (or a good job), Angela wasn't sure where that money would come from. To make a long story short, she earned a $375 cash grant from her school a few weeks into the drive because of her good grades. She was excited to add that to the money she already had to reach her missions giving goal! (Pause.)

Stop and think about what you would do if you didn't have the money to pay for college and you received a grant to further your education. An opportunity to get ahead, right? In most cases that's exactly how you should view it. But in this case, that's not what Angela felt like God wanted her to do. She gladly gave the money away! (Play.)

I received an email from Angela recently and was blown away by her incredible spirit. Giving that $400 offering literally meant that she might not be able to register for classes the following semester. Amazingly, that wasn't her first concern. In the email, she was quick to mention how excited she was about the kids who would hear about Jesus because of her participation in the missions project. One line jumped off the page when I read it: "I would rather give to them than go to school next semester, if that is the case." Wow—that's contentment!

I don't know what next semester is going to look like for Angela. Last I checked, she didn't either. One thing is for certain: As I've studied Scripture and attempted to live a life of overflow,

I've discovered that when you take care of God's business He takes care of yours. Angela is going to experience overflow because she's committed to contentment. Even if it means her educational plans get delayed a semester, she is committed to living a life of generosity. That's one of the reasons I'm confident that God has big plans for Angela and that He's going to provide for her step-by-step as those plans unfold. I can't wait to see how He honors her commitment and generosity. He'll do the same for you as you learn to embrace contentment.

I really enjoyed this email from Zack (aka "Z-FUNK!"), a high school student at Realife. In addition to being one of the most hilarious guys I know, Zack has really demonstrated a commitment to contentment through our recent missions project:

Yo Scotty G!!!

Hey bro this is my/God's story! I was praying and thinking on what I could give at the beginning of the drive. I work at paid childcare at the church and I get about $20 every two weeks. And with paying for gas and food I just didn't know how much I could truly give! So I felt God laying on my heart $20 a week, so that's what I wrote down. I would give $20 a week, that would be double of what I make and I couldn't drive anywhere or eat anything!!!!!! Ha ha! Butcha gotta have faith!!!

So through the drive I was starting to get a little freaked out because I had only raised $40 and time was running out! I knew Christmas was coming up and my parents always go all out for me! (They're awesome parents!!!!) I sat them down and asked if for Christmas this year they could just give me the money they were going to spend on my presents for [missions]. And at first they were a little iffy about it but they thought it was a pretty cool idea in the end and agreed to it. Tonight on the way to church my mom and I stopped at the bank and she got $200 out for me!!! So that added to my $40 I had already met and exceeded my goal!!! Then I remembered my parents and I saved our change over the 11 week drive and had $9.45 in pennies, nickels, dimes, and quarters! (I asked Dylan Nuckolls for 55 cents just to make it even.) With faith and hard work I exceeded my goal by $30!!! God is so good!! Oh yeah and when I decided to give my Christmas to [missions] I had told some of my unsaved friends about it and they were so amazed that they are going to buy me something for Christmas!! So to sum it all up God is sooooooooooooooo good!!!

Your boy,
Z-FUNK!

Are you experiencing overflow yet? Are you satisfied with what you have? If the answer is yes, then you're well on your way to an overflowing existence—just like Zack. Zack understands contentment; he has this A-OK outlook on life that doesn't depend on what he does or doesn't have at any given moment. If you're not there yet, hang in there; this is a marathon, not a sprint!

God helped the apostle Paul to be content in crazy circumstances; He is able to help you too.

Zack and Angela's stories aren't just about being content. Zack's eagerness to give up his Christmas gifts and Angela's willingness to put her life on hold are ultimately possible because of faith. Contentment is great, "butcha gotta have faith!!!" as Zack so eloquently stated in his email. Believe it or not (and it would be fitting for you to believe it), our next chapter is all about faith (and a few teenagers with rocking chairs)!

Did You Know ...

The average home in the U.S. now has more television sets than people to sit down and watch them. More than 50% of American homes have at least three working televisions; the average home has 2.8 TVs!

(Nielsen Media Research, September 2006, *USA Today*)

application questions

1. Can you think of any recent examples where you heard someone complaining because they weren't content in one way or another? How could they have changed their perspective to be grateful?

2. Typically, do others view you as someone who is content or as someone who is never satisfied with what they have? Why?

3. Who in your life models godly contentment that you can look to as an example?

4. Since we know that contentment is a key to enjoying life, how can you develop a content heart?

5. In this chapter, Scotty explains why contentment is important, offering a couple of reasons. List some of the other benefits that come with living a life of contentment.

5

faith

We live by faith, not by sight.
2 Corinthians 5:7

Faith can lead us to do some crazy things, things that otherwise are … well … unexplainable! I don't know how else to introduce what Drew, Daniel, and Dean did to raise money for our missions project. These three amigos raised money for missions by holding what they promoted as a "rock-a-thon."

With a name like "rock-a-thon," you might imagine a Guitar Hero tournament to benefit missions or maybe a Battle of the Bands competition—but you'd be wrong! With permission (and that's an important little detail), these three jokers took rocking chairs to Incredible Pizza Company, one of our city's busiest attractions. On any given Saturday, this place is packed with people, so that's when these guys set up their chairs outside the entrance and took donations for rocking. They rocked … back … and forth … back … and forth … for 12 (yes, 12) hours straight! These guys were definitely motivated by faith and not feelings because they spent six of those hours rocking outside in 40-degree weather! I don't know that I would've been able to handle that. I think I would've called it the "rock-n-roll"—I would rock as long as it was 60 degrees and sunny and roll right out of there about the time I started to see my breath!

Seriously, though, what these guys did took some major faith! Sitting outside and rocking in the winter isn't exactly a walk in the park (it's more of a rock on the sidewalk). But Drew, Daniel, and Dean trusted that God would provide if they stepped out in faith. They trusted God as they tried to figure out how in the world to transport three huge rocking chairs across town. They trusted God in that first moment on the parking lot, the one where they could easily have been tempted to second guess themselves—"are we really going to unload these rocking chairs in front of all of these people?" They trusted God as they rocked and raised money for missions. And God responded powerfully to Drew, Daniel, and Dean's faith. In just one day, these guys rocked in $500 to support missionaries! I apologize in advance for what I'm about to write, but that rocks!

The life of faith is so much fun! But it can also be scary.

I think back to the response time after youth service on the second night of our drive. A lot of students stayed in the auditorium to pray long after the service was over, asking God to help them reach the goals that He'd placed on their hearts. For many students, the amount God challenged them to give was far beyond what they felt they were able to do. I remember praying with a high school student named Kyle. He fought back tears as he showed me his journal—he had scratched through his original goal of $700. That number was overwhelming enough, but Kyle felt like God was saying He had something even bigger planned. I saw where he had written his increased goal of $1,000! Kyle had no idea how he was going to be able to give so much in such a short amount of time. What he did have, though, was faith—he knew that God was able to help and trusted that He would.

When Kyle's dad heard about his goal, he offered to donate the first ten percent. A lot of kids would've jumped at that head start, but not Kyle. He felt like God wanted to stretch his faith. He thanked his dad, and politely turned him down. I think that is so amazing! Over the next few weeks, God worked powerfully in response to Kyle's faith. I loved reading the email he sent me that detailed how time after time after time, God came through in response to Kyle's faith. And Kyle's faith is active; he definitely did his part.

Kyle works with wood and makes these incredibly beautiful hand-carved bowls. He was able to sell some of his work and donated the money from the sales to missions. He also worked extra hours at his job when he could. It was so cool to hear how in one of his paychecks, Kyle received some bonuses that were completely unexpected. Kyle stepped out in faith and God helped him blow his goal out of the water. In total, he gave more than $1,000 in less than three months—almost twice his original goal!

Some people have this weird idea that the life of a Christian is boring. Nothing could be further from the truth! Living for God is an unbelievably exciting adventure.

We don't live like the rest of the world, relying only on our natural senses. We have a supernatural connection to a powerful God who is actively involved in our lives! When you step out in faith—when you decide to dream a big dream and do a big thing for God—you're in for the most exhilarating, adrenalin-rushing experience of your life!

Nothing is more important in your life as a Christian than your faith, an unshakable trust in our rock-solid God!

That same confidence is critical if you're going to experience an overflowing life. There are all kinds of things that could be said about faith, but as it relates to giving, I want to quickly point out two aspects of faith: dependence and confidence.

The first aspect of faith is dependence—the belief that God knows what you need and is able to provide it, combined with the willingness to trust that He will. You could say that this is the more passive aspect of faith. In this sense, faith is a resting in the fact that God is going to take care of you. It's a recognition that everything you have comes from Him. You can depend on God to take care of you!

That doesn't mean you don't have a responsibility to work for the money you earn. You certainly do have a responsibility, but it's not the same kind of work as you would see in the life of someone who doesn't believe in God—a stressful, make-or-break kind of work that is driven by a growing greed for more. As a follower of Christ you work hard, but you recognize that the results aren't up to you. One of the Proverbs puts it this way: "The horse is made ready for the day of battle, but victory rests with the Lord" (Proverbs 21:31). In other words, you give your best and depend on God to take care of the rest.

In the Sermon on the Mount, Jesus talks about the incredible beauty of wildflowers to illustrate the importance of dependence. He points out that the flowers of the field don't worry about making themselves—well—flowery. God has all of that under control.

Jesus then compares us to those wildflowers: "If God gives such attention to the appearance of wildflowers—most of which are never even seen—don't you think he'll attend to you, take pride in you, do his best for you? What I'm trying to do here is to get you to relax, to not be so preoccupied with *getting*, so you can respond to God's *giving*. People who don't know God and the way he works fuss over these things, but you know both God and how he works. Steep your life in God-reality, God-initiative, God-provisions. Don't worry about missing out. You'll find all your everyday human concerns will be met" (Matthew 6:30-33, *The Message*).

The second aspect of faith is confidence—the belief that God wants to do something great in and through you, combined with a willingness to be used for His glory. This is the active aspect of faith. Where dependence is a resting in the fact that God is going to take care of you, confidence leads to an active participation in God's will and work.

Faith isn't just some flowery idea! It's a radical lifestyle where we live, not according to what we see, but by what we know to be true.

The truth of the matter is that God saved you so that He could work in and through you for His glory. God's plan for you is incredible! He's able to do exceeding abundantly beyond all that you could ask or imagine (Ephesians 3:20)! Those truths from God's Word should inspire a confident faith in your heart that leads you to the cutting edge of what God is doing.

As a youth pastor, I love working with students because they are so filled with faith! Often, the life of faith is new to them, or it's something that they are taking personal ownership of for the first time. Given the opportunity, teenagers often embrace giving not just with dependence but with confidence. They realize that there is no limit to what God might do in and through them, whether its scary (like a $1,000 goal) or hilarious (like a rock-a-thon for missions).

Check out what Jesus says about this kind of confident faith: "Embrace this God-life. Really embrace it, and nothing will be too much for you. This mountain, for instance: Just say, 'Go jump in the lake'—no shuffling or shilly-shallying—and it's as good as done. That's why I urge you to pray for absolutely everything, ranging from small to large. Include everything as you embrace this God-life, and you'll get God's everything" (Mark 11:22-24, *The Message*).

This isn't some Sunday-School faith. This is jump-out-of-the-boat-and-walk-on-water faith! The overflowing life is the life of faith—a life lived on the edge of God's plan in an absolutely unpredictable day-by-day adventure. In the next chapter, we're going to see how my friend Trenton started experiencing that adventure of faith as a regular part of his everyday lifestyle.

Did You Know...

On average, teens 14-17 spend $46.80 per mall visit! They visit malls more frequently than any other age group—averaging once per week—and also spend the most time per visit.

(*Teen Market Profile 2004*)

application questions

1. What is one big dream that you have when it comes to missions giving this year?

2. What excites you about living a life of faith?

3. What actions need to be taken to go from dreaming a big dream to doing a big thing for God?

4. Who are some friends that can help you to accomplish your dreams for this year?

5. How do you think God will honor you for the faith you show through giving?

6

lifestyle

Where your treasure is,
there your heart will be also.
Luke 12:34

When I travel and speak, I really enjoy taking a young leader
with me—usually someone who senses that God is calling
them to student ministry. It's a great opportunity to hang out
and talk about ministry. It's always a lot of fun. This summer,
my friend Trenton joined me at our district's summer camp.
I was the camp speaker that week and was planning on
preaching a message about giving in one of the sessions. While
I was preparing for that message, I asked Trenton if, as a
student, he had ever personally seen God do something great
in response to his stepping out in faith and giving sacrificially.

"Absolutely," he said. "One night at Realife, you shared the story of the missionary needing a vehicle. My heart was gripped and I knew I needed to do something. When I prayed and asked God how much He wanted me to give, there was a number that kept coming to my mind. I thought it must just be my imagination, because there was no way I could come up with that much money on my own. But sure enough, by the end of the drive, God worked a miracle and I was able to meet my goal of $300."

"Wow, that's awesome!" I replied. Curious as to how his miracle had happened I asked Trenton about the details. "How did God provide? Was it a check in the mail? Did a stranger show up with a cash-filled envelope and disappear before you could look up?"

I was both surprised and impressed by Trenton's response: "When I started trying to pay my pledge, I realized that I didn't even have enough money to meet my weekly goal. And that's when God did it … He gave me a job. I knew God had answered me. He had placed the number on my heart that He wanted me to give and then He gave me the job so I could earn the money."

That's right, God provided for Trenton through his job as a life guard. And although he didn't jump into the pool to save a single life that summer, he earned his paychecks just the same. The lives he was saving were those of people he would never meet.

I was so impressed by his maturity and his perspective on giving that I asked Trenton to share his story with the camp. That night, the camp collected the largest offering in its history. I'm glad Trenton stepped out in faith and did his part. Not only did he hit his goal, but his generosity overflowed to inspire hundreds of students to do the same.

It's been said that money makes the world go 'round. Money is the reason businesses everywhere open their doors every day. Sure, they have other goals. For instance, some businesses provide a product—that nifty something-or-other that you can't live without (or don't want to live without). Other businesses provide services like accounting or dry cleaning or graphic design. Either way, the goal of a business is to make moolah. All of these organizations are supported financially by individuals like you and me. In turn, they support the economies of the nations around the world. In that sense, money is what makes the world work at the most basic level.

Now that we're all caught up to speed on economics, let's get a little bit more personal. Money isn't just a powerful force in our world; it's a powerful force in your life. I don't mean that money is your motivation or pursuit in life. It shouldn't be and we'll cover that later. I am suggesting, though, that money is central to your earthly experience. Think for a minute about how much of your life is affected by finances.

Let's start at work. Perhaps you are the master of the grill at an independently-owned franchise diner. Translation: you flip burgers at Mickey D's. Why do you go to work bright and early every Saturday morning? I suppose it could be for the 10% discount you get on those delicious apple pies that come in the little cardboard sleeves. Or maybe you find deep satisfaction serving up McMuffins with a smile. Now, I may be going out on a limb here, but I'm guessing that neither of those things motivates you to wake up bright and early every Saturday for your McJob. Let's be honest: you're there for the McDollars!

Money is the most practical reason that we spend a third of our lives at work. If we didn't have to earn money, we would find plenty of other things to do with all of that time! The reason we don't is because we have to earn money to buy the things we need. After all, money directly affects your lifestyle—where you live, how you dress, and what you do for fun (to name just a few things). Finances affect big decisions like where you'll go to college and little decisions like what you'll do tonight for dinner. Like it or not, money affects almost every aspect of your earthly life, which is why it's so important that you have a healthy perspective on it!

Some people think that money is evil, but there's nothing wrong with money in and of itself. It's neither good nor bad.

It can, however, be used to do good or bad. For example, you could give a thousand dollars to one person and they'd use it to feed the homeless. You could give that same amount to someone else and they'd use it to pay the family of a suicide bomber. That same thousand dollars might be used yet again by someone else to buy—I don't know—an extensive collection of Chia Pets.

Where people go wrong with money is allowing greed into their heart and life. Nothing will keep you from experiencing an overflowing life like greed will. That's why Paul warned Timothy that "the love of money is a root of all kinds of evil" (1 Timothy 6:10). If we're not careful, we can place our trust or confidence in the security that we think our money (or our parents' money) gives us. But the security money provides isn't real: "Cast but a glance at riches, and they are gone," Proverbs 23:5 says, "for they will surely sprout wings and fly off to the sky like an eagle."

God understands how much money can influence our lives. That's why He talks about it so often in the Bible.

In fact, the Bible has more to say about money than about any other topic. God cares deeply about the details of our lives— even our finances! One of my favorite verses about money is a quote from Jesus. In the book of Luke, he says something that is both simple and profound: "… where your treasure is, there your heart will be also" (Luke 12:34).

I love how relevant the Bible is to our everyday life! Jesus, speaking 2,000 years before the modern stock market or MTV Cribs, cuts to the heart of one of the key issues facing Christians in twenty-first century America. He pushes past the periphery and sums up the most important thing Christians need to know about money in their lives: where your treasure is, there your heart will be also. Jesus is saying that your heart and life are intertwined with—wrapped up in—the things you treasure. I love how *The Message* phrases it: "The place where your treasure is, is the place you will most want to be, and end up being."

Simply put, the things you treasure will determine your desires, and ultimately, the course of your life. You can spend your life pursuing money and you'll wind up empty on the inside (even if you're not empty-handed). It's possible to have more than you could ever want or need materially and be absolutely bankrupt spiritually. For example, if you do a little research, you'll find that many lottery winners end up wishing they had never bought that "lucky" ticket. Why? When your heart's not in the right place, money doesn't solve your problems; it actually compounds them! On the other hand, you can choose to treasure the things that are important to God. You can pursue a generous life. Before long, you'll experience the joy and benefits of overflow!

I want to tell you about two girls who learned to make giving a lifestyle over the course of this missions project. As exciting as it is to hit a numerical goal, what's even more exciting is learning to live a lifestyle of generosity that will last past any temporary drive or project. That's what happened for Liz, a high school student at Realife. Over the course of the project, things didn't exactly work out for Liz the way she thought they would. She tried getting different jobs, but nothing panned out. The money wasn't coming in. Then, seemingly out of nowhere, Liz was confronted with some personal challenges that were difficult and distracting to say the least.

Liz sat in youth service on the final night of the missions project, realizing that she had given less money than she had initially hoped. But God was still at work in her heart! As Liz listened to a handful of her friends tell the youth group about their giving experiences—about good times and bad, about big victories and little—she sensed that God was speaking to her about making generosity a lifestyle. Liz later told me in an email that she realized that just because the project stopped, her giving didn't have to—generosity would become her lifestyle. That's what really matters!

Kayla is a high school student who earns about $60 on a good week. Over the course of the project, God helped Kayla to give more than $600 to missions! One of the cool things about Kayla's story is that she reached her goal by thinking very carefully about her lifestyle. She gave every penny she earned from her job. She sold things to raise money. She gave up meals. When her friends went to see a movie, she passed. God certainly doesn't expect Kayla to live like that for the rest of her life, but the lesson that she learned through the experience is incredibly valuable—God can do great things if we will give him every detail of our lives!

You've made it this far, so I'm assuming you want to experience the kind of overflowing life that Liz and Kayla now know firsthand—you want to be rich toward God. So, what does that look like in your everyday life? You want to treasure the things of God because you want your heart to be His completely, but how do you make sure that's happening practically?

The answer is really pretty simple. It comes down to a lifestyle that you choose to live. Your lifestyle is made up of all of the little decisions you make everyday—in this case, we're focusing on your financial decisions. So, let's start with your paycheck or allowance. When you get it, what do you do with it? If you're wondering where your treasure is, take a look at where your money is going. God asks us to give the first ten percent of our income to Him as an act of worship called the "tithe" (you can read more about tithing in Malachi 3).

God asks for the first portion of our income as a reminder that all that we have comes from Him. He lets us decide what we do with the other ninety percent. (I'd say that's a pretty good deal!)

Does that mean that you can blow the other ninety percent? Not if you want to experience overflow! The extent to which God will overflow in your life is directly related to your generosity. If you want to experience a little overflow, then give just a little bit beyond the ten percent God requires. If you want to experience a lot of overflow, then give a lot.

Beyond the tithe, there are all kinds of opportunities for you to be generous. You can stretch your faith by giving to missionaries who need money so they can go around the world and fulfill their calling to preach the gospel. You can bless those who are less fortunate in your community—those who are poor or who might be going through a difficult time. You could give to a special project at your church, like a building campaign. You could give to causes of compassion around the world—rebuilding communities after natural disasters, drilling clean water wells for the thirsty, rescuing children from sex trafficking. There is no shortage of opportunities to give! What you do is less important than the fact that you do something—that you take action—that you live your lifestyle in such a way that God's generosity overflows through you.

Let me encourage you to do some research to find out about the different opportunities there are to give. Think about it, pray about it, and then do something about it. If it's going to make a difference—if you're going to overflow—giving has to become your lifestyle. You may have to give up the daily drink from that friendly neighborhood coffee shop. It might mean that you sell some stuff on eBay. It may even require you to say no to some commitments to make room for others. Whatever your situation, it won't take you long to think of several ways that you can start to make overflow your lifestyle.

In the next chapter, you're going to hear about the student who gave the most over the course of our 11-week missions project. Read on and find out what he did when his parents told him that selling his car wasn't the best way to hit his goal!

Did You Know ...

The top 10 items teenagers recently purchased are: 1) clothes; 2) food; 3) candy/soda or soft drinks; 4) salty snacks/CD or recorded music; 5) lunch; 6) shoes; 7) video games; 8) jewelry; 9) magazines; 10) ice cream.

(*Teen Market Profile 2004*)

application questions

1. How do true stories of how God helps others encourage you to live a generous life?

2. Who will you share your overflow story with to encourage them to be a giver?

3. When it comes to money, how are your habits? What can you do to improve your weaknesses in this area?

4. What are some ways that you can practice generosity with your life and money?

5. How can generosity become a habit or lifestyle, a permanent part of who you are as a person?

attitude

God loves a cheerful giver.
2 Corinthians 9:7

I want you to read an email I received from Josh, the individual student who gave the most money during Realife's missions drive. As you read it, pay attention to all of the details that are indicators of Josh's incredible attitude:

Hey Scotty,

During this drive, my focus was to give all I could in order to glorify Jesus; I just wanted to do something big and glorify Him! I didn't do anything fancy or outrageous that would make people really think I was something, but I sure gave my all in the fact that I was going to glorify the Lord anyway I could.

My parents knew about what I was wanting to do for the Lord and offered to pay me if I cleaned the house each week (something they knew I absolutely despised doing) ... but I of course took the offer with the enthusiasm of knowing people's lives were going to be changed, which made the cleaning a lot more easy! During the eleven weeks of my "cleaning campaign," I as well was holding out on lunches and giving my lunch money instead (I basically did this four out of the five school days each week). As well, there would be times where my parents would give me money for food on weekends and/or if I was going to be hanging out with friends, and if my parents told me to hold on to the change, I would collect that as well. I also would mention the cause at FCA [Fellowship of Christian Athletes] each Friday where we would get an occasional giver. And my friend, Tyler, has an uncle that works for a fundraising company and we no doubt went that route and sold some cookie dough and a ton of other desserts for Jesus!

Like I said, there was nothing fancy about what I did other than the fact that God did bless my best while raising $1,383 for His glory! God's heart isn't for the money being given, it's for the people's lives being changed! His will isn't for us to give in order to show off the amount of money we gave, His will is that we would give in order to glorify His name, enhance His kingdom, and encourage other brothers and sisters in the body of Christ to do the same! We serve one awesome King that is worthy of our best! So let's give it to Him!

Alright, my friend, I'm about to head to the church in a bit, where I shall see you. Throw down tonight! Love you and praying for you.

Josh

I love being around Josh because he's got an incredible attitude that energizes everything that he does!

What Josh didn't mention in his email is that in addition to everything else he did throughout the course of this missions project, he also tried to sell his car and a very important guitar. Wow! When his parents exercised their spiritual authority and encouraged Josh to find other ways to give, he put his good attitude to hard work (even though he didn't exactly love the cleaning ministry). With God's help, he gave more than any other student! As a side note, I want to put out something that's really important. Josh honored his parents' spiritual authority with a great attitude, and God blessed him as a result. When you honor your parents, God will honor you!

Think of the best gift you've ever received. It could have been a birthday present or maybe a Christmas gift. Maybe there wasn't even a special occasion. It could be that you received something completely unexpected that caught you by surprise. I don't know for sure (after all, I wasn't there), but there's a good chance that the person who gave you this gift may have been even more excited about giving it than you were about receiving it. Haven't you noticed that's the way it works? After all, Jesus said that it's more blessed to give than to receive (Acts 20:35).

Now, imagine how you would have felt if the person who gave you that special little something offered it to you with an apathetic look on their face. "Here, take it," they say. "Go on … open it already. Let's get this over with!"

As you start to unwrap the "gift," the giver explains their sentiments: "I had to get you something. I knew you would've been really upset if I hadn't. I'm just glad I found this on clearance. Now I can finally check you off the list! I hope you like it—but if not, let me know because I wouldn't mind getting my money back."

I bet that's not exactly the scene you imagined when you thought of the best gift you've ever received. An attitude like that would make even the coolest gift seem lame! After all, giving is supposed to be fun for all involved, the recipient and the giver. It should be life-giving! It should make you smile! It's meant to be an act of celebration!

Giving to God is the same way. There should be nothing more exciting than offering your resources back to God and sensing the smile of his heart. You wouldn't want to receive a gift that was given halfheartedly. You wouldn't think of offering a halfhearted gift to a friend or family member. And yet, that's the way a lot of people give to God!

In 2 Corinthians 9:7, Paul says that "God loves a cheerful giver."

God's not as concerned about our actual gifts as He is the attitude with which we give them. He doesn't need our gifts. God has unlimited resources; He asks us to give because we need to learn to be generous, not because He needs something from us.

What's really cool about God is that He doesn't just point the way and command us to give. He has set an incredible example for us. The Bible says that Jesus is an "indescribable gift" (2 Corinthians 9:15). One of the first verses of Scripture that you probably ever learned (or saw on a sign at an NFL game) says that God loved the world so much that He gave us His Son (John 3:16). Jesus offered us his life as a gift, wrapped in an attitude of love.

I've found that a great attitude toward giving is a natural overflow of the heart when you understand that it's an expression of worship to God.

In Luke 7, Jesus knows that He's going to the cross within about a week's time. As He is thinking about the fact that He's going to be pouring out His life to save sinners, a notorious sinner selflessly pours out a pint of perfume on Him in an extravagant expression of worship. In case you're wondering why this lady is dousing Jesus with perfume, allow me to offer a little bit of explanation (because it may seem a little weird by today's cultural standards).

In those days, people didn't have many of the modern luxuries that we enjoy today—luxuries like … funeral homes. As a child, maybe you saw the flannel board version of Lazarus being raised from the dead; if so, you understand that basically they used to wrap dead people up in Charmin two-ply. If a family was really wealthy, they might use the Quilted Northern jumbo roll. OK, not really! But, when someone did die in Jesus' day, his or her body was often anointed with perfume to help control the less-than-pleasant odor. Jesus later explained that the woman's gift was an act of worship—she was preparing the Son of God for burial by covering Him with perfume.

Her act of worship is exceptionally beautiful if you stop and think about it. First of all, she poured out a pint of expensive perfume with abandon. She didn't hold any of it back! Now, we're not talking about a bottle of Chanel here—something she picked up at JCPenney. Perfume would've been a hot commodity back in the day. This was incredibly valuable stuff, worth a year's wages! The thought of its value apparently hadn't entered her mind. Or if it had, she must have recognized that Jesus deserved infinitely more than the most valuable gift she had to offer.

Can you imagine what this gift must have meant to Jesus? As He lived out His final days on this earth, the fragrance of her gift was a reminder to Jesus of the attitude of a worshipper. I don't know about you, but I want my giving to be characterized by that kind of enthusiastic extravagance. I want my generosity to be a sweet-smelling fragrance to God!

God is looking at the heart that motivates your giving. Do you give cheerfully or do you go through the dull motions of duty? God doesn't need your money. What He desires is an authentic expression of worship. As we'll see in the next chapter, some of the most powerful expressions of worshipful giving are those that are the most costly.

Did You Know ...

Over a third of teens hold part-time jobs, working 18 hours a week on average, and earning $483 per month. They are using their disposable income first and foremost for clothes, followed by eating out, cars, movies and cell phones.

(2006 Harrison Group/*VNU Teen Trend Report*, Nov. 2006)

application questions

1. Read through the first email by Josh again, and notice how many times he mentions his desire to give God glory. Would you say your attitude is similar to Josh's when it comes to giving? Why or why not?

2. When you give of your finances is it out of joy or out of obligation?

3. If you were to give a gift to God, what do you think He would want?

4. Do you think God is honored more by your gift or the attitude in giving that gift?

5. How can you demonstrate a godly attitude in your giving that will inspire others to give?

8

sacrifice

Out of the most severe trial,
their overflowing joy and their extreme poverty
welled up in rich generosity.
2 Corinthians 8:2

I collapsed onto the couch in my office after a Wednesday
night youth service, exhausted from preaching (preceded by a
full day's work). One of my friends sat in the chair across the
room and we talked about all that God was doing through
Realife's missions project and how amazed we were at it
all. As the conversation moved along, we talked about the
different sacrifices that students were so courageously making
in order to give to missions. Two of those stories really stood
out to me.

Ellie is a student leader at Realife who wanted to make some sort of sacrifice so that she could give more to missions. Throughout the 11-week drive, she regularly skipped lunch at school and gave the money that she would've spent on food to missions. Ellie later explained with humility that she didn't think of her actions as overly sacrificial: "We have it so good. We are blessed. The little things I did to raise money are nothing compared to what missionaries do every day to take the gospel to others." Thanks to Ellie's attitude and sacrifice, those missionaries have more of the resources that they need to effectively fulfill their calling!

We talked about how cool it was that Ellie was willing to sacrifice meals so she could give even more generously. Then it was quiet for a minute. Wednesdays are long days, and my friend and I were both really tired. All of a sudden, I remembered Michael and Ben's story. "Have you heard it yet?" I asked. He hadn't, so I started to fill him in.

Both of these guys come from large families and, as is the case for a lot of us, there's not a lot of extra money lying around the house. But that didn't stop them from giving sacrificially! Michael and Ben organized two "walk-a-thons," where they collected money from people who sponsored them for every mile they walked. During their first walk-a-thon, these guys walked 30 miles! In case you're a little unclear on distances, get this: they walked for 12 hours straight (taking only minor breaks to use the restroom)! We talked about how Michael and Ben were incredibly sore at 26 miles, ready to call it quits. But then they talked about how far the money that they would raise in the last four miles would go on the mission field—and kept on trucking! These guys also organized a second walk-a-thon when the temperature outside was a freezing 32 degrees (and you already know how I feel about that)!

When it was all said and done, these guys gave more than $600 to missions because of their willingness to sacrifice!

I've got to mention one other person in this chapter on sacrifice. David Grant isn't a student at Realife, though he spoke to the group at one of the youth services during our missions drive. This guy is a hero in the faith! Over the course of his life and ministry, he's raised countless dollars for missions efforts around the world! If you've ever had the privilege of hearing him speak, then you know his remarkable story. Captivated by God's calling on his life to share the gospel throughout India, David gave every dollar that he made until the age of 30 to missions! Every dollar! It doesn't get much more sacrificial than that! It would take a book a lot larger than this one to adequately explain the impact that David Grant has had for the cause of Christ. What I want you to understand is that the fact that he's experienced such incredible overflow in his life and ministry is not accidental. It's the result of a lifetime of sacrifice.

These stories remind me of a moving story of sacrifice from Mark's gospel: "Jesus sat down opposite the place where the offerings were put and watched the crowd putting their money into the temple treasury. Many rich people threw in large amounts. But a poor widow came and put in two very small copper coins, worth only a fraction of a penny. Calling his disciples to him, Jesus said, 'I tell you the truth, this poor widow has put more into the treasury than all the others. They all gave out of their wealth; but she, out of her poverty, put in everything—all she had to live on'" (Mark 12:41-44).

When you read stories like these, it makes you realize that God isn't interested in the bottom line dollar amount of our offerings. We read in the last chapter that God is looking at our attitude, but what we're learning here is that He's also paying attention to the extent of our sacrifice. As Americans who are abundantly blessed, we rarely make sacrifices that are worthy of the word (if we're honest). When we think about making "sacrifices," we think about things like living without cable TV, eating at home instead of eating out, or deciding against buying another winter coat and making do with the two we already own. We may be giving some things up, but they aren't really sacrifices!

If you're like me, you probably realize there's more you could sacrifice. Let me encourage you that it's OK for your giving to grow with time.

One of the things you'll notice as you start to experience overflow at work in your own life, is that God will lead you to step out in faith in greater and greater ways. Your journey of generosity may start out with you giving up a couple of coffees a week to sponsor a kid in Africa—that's great! But as you mature in your perspective and as your faith grows, God will progressively bring you to a place of more sacrificial giving—a place that may not be comfortable financially, a place where it may even hurt to give!

I have to admit that in my own life, giving has been a growth process. My wife, Casey, and I have stepped out in faith financially several times over the years. We'd set a giving goal, God would help us meet it, and He would always bless us in return in one way or another. With each opportunity to give, we've stepped out in faith a little more. Actually, it's felt like we've stepped out in faith a lot more these last few years! Let's just say that Casey is always ready and willing to give—she has this amazing ability to see an opportunity almost everywhere—but it often takes me a little while to catch up to her faith!

I can't say that I know yet what it means to sacrifice in the sense David Grant knows it or the widow knew it. But I'm learning. And, honestly, I can say that I'm loving it! I've learned to trust God when He asks us to make a sacrifice, because He always uses it to do something greater than I could have imagined!

All of this talk about sacrifice reminds me of Jim Elliot, a missionary who was martyred in 1956 while sharing the gospel with the Auca Indians in Ecuador. The Aucas (also called the Huaorani Indians), were a violent tribe who had very limited contact with the outside world (and had never heard the gospel) until Elliot and his brave team of missionaries sought them out. Jim Elliot's story is incredible; if you haven't read it, you should! Some years before Jim and three of his fellow missionaries were killed, he wrote something in his journal that really puts this idea of sacrifice into perspective: "He is no fool who gives what he cannot keep to gain that which he cannot lose." That is one of my all-time favorite quotes in the world!

When you give financially (or in Elliot's case, when you give your life), you're sacrificing something that you ultimately can't keep anyway.

The amazing thing is that as a result, you're gaining something that you cannot lose. In addition to the eternal reward that Elliot is experiencing today, nearly all of the Auca Indian tribe came to know Christ as a result of his sacrifice and that of his friends. Beyond that, Jim Elliot literally inspired an entire generation of young missionaries who would go on to do incredible things for God around the world—now that's overflow! And none of it would've happened, if it weren't for sacrifice.

Only God knows what He may call you or me to sacrifice; what I do know is that the reward will be well worth it—a lesson I learned from my dad …

Did You Know …

If you gave up your morning coffee run (at an average of $3 a pop) and instead put three dollars a day in an account making 8%, you would have $134,000 after 30 years!

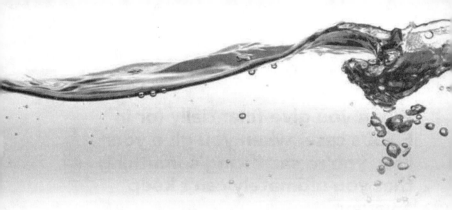

application questions

1. What are some small financial sacrifices that you can make to increase your giving to missions?

2. What are some small comforts that you could sacrifice to increase your giving to missions?

3. Are your answers to questions 1 and 2 really sacrifices?

4. Is your sacrifice more like the widow who gave her all out of the little she had, or like those who gave little out of their abundance?

5. How does Jim Elliot's quote, "He is no fool who gives what he cannot keep to gain that which he cannot lose," motivate you to start sacrificing more?

9

reward

Whoever sows generously
will also reap generously.
2 Corinthians 9:6

"Pastor Scotty, will you draw the name?" Alicia was holding a huge bowl filled with folded up pieces of paper. For the last few weeks, she had been coordinating a drawing at school, selling her friends an opportunity to win an iPod. This wasn't just any iPod—it was the iPod Alicia was going to be getting for Christmas. Instead, she asked her parents if she could donate the little music maker to raise money for missions. They agreed and Alicia went to work!

Before I drew the name out of the bowl to see who won, Alicia told me that one of the hundreds of tickets in there had been bought by her brother. He had told her that if he won the iPod, he would give it to her, since she had been willing to give it away so selflessly.

I stuck my hand in the bowl, dug around, picked a name, and pulled it out. Alicia looked at me, wondering which of her friends would be going home with a little love from Apple. I opened the piece of paper slowly for dramatic effect. I looked up at Alicia with wide eyes.

"It's your brother!" I could barely believe it. This was definitely a God-moment!

Alicia snatched the paper from my hands, wanting to see it for herself. It looked like she might cry. "God gave me my iPod back!"

I was so happy for Alicia, and not just because she would now be rockin' out with a new MP3 player. She was learning a lesson in overflow. She had let go of her iPod so that God could work through her to raise money for missions. And He did; Alicia brought in $450! And after all was said and done, God rewarded her! Alicia got her iPod back, and with it an incredible experience that she will remember every time she starts to unravel the headphones.

Did you know that the Bible clearly teaches that God rewards generosity?

Paul says it this way in Galatians: "we reap what we sow" (Galatians 6:7, paraphrased). Now, just to make sure there's no confusion, this verse isn't referring to the stitching together of fabric with thread. The concept actually comes from farming—the word *sow* means "to plant" and the word *reap* means "to gather." The idea is that if you plant a seed of corn, you can expect to harvest a crop of corn. It's the way life works and it's called "the law of the harvest."

Each time you give, you're sowing seed. It's like you're making an investment. And as you'll soon see, you can expect to reap a reward (a return on that investment) as a result. Receiving a reward shouldn't be our motivation for giving, of course—if you're unclear on that, you may want to review Chapter 6—and yet, the law of the harvest is undeniable. God rewards us in response to our giving!

John Lindell, my pastor and friend, has shared a great message over the years to teach our church about the law of the harvest. It's been amazing to see the blessing that God has poured out as our congregation has embraced this truth! In his message, John explains three really cool truths about sowing and reaping:

1. We reap *what* we sow.

If you were to plant a tomato seed in a certain spot in your garden, you would be really surprised if a corn stalk grew up in its place. Why? Because you reap *what* you sow. If you sow kindness, you're going to reap kindness in your relationships. If you sow bitterness, you are going to reap bitterness (and may not have too many meaningful relationships as a result). The same principle holds true with our finances. When we give away our money, it has a way of finding its way back to us. If you're generous with your money, you can expect to be blessed financially in return!

2. We reap *after* we sow.

A farmer would be considered krazy (that's right, crazy with a k) if he tried to gather a harvest before he planted any seed. Why? Because you reap *after* you sow. You may feel like you don't have the money to live generously. Maybe you plan on waiting to give until you have more money to do so. Let me encourage you to give what you can now, even if it's just a little bit. You'll be amazed to see how God blesses you after you do!

3. We reap *more than* we sow.

Farming wouldn't be a very profitable occupation if every time you planted a seed, you harvested just one in return. Thankfully, that's not the way it works! By planting just one kernel of corn, you can expect to get hundreds of kernels when you take in your crop. Why? Because you reap *more than* you sow. When you step out in faith and give, you'll be astounded at how God blesses you back more generously than you deserve!

The old saying may be a little corny, but it's true: "you can't out-give God"!

The apostle Paul understood the law of the harvest. That's why he challenged the Corinthian church to give by explaining to them that their generosity (or lack of it) would come back to affect them directly: "Remember this: Whoever sows sparingly will also reap sparingly, and whoever sows generously will also reap generously" (2 Corinthians 9:6). If you want to be rewarded generously, then give generously!

As with almost anything else, this principle can be taken to an unhealthy extreme. I'd encourage you to guard your heart against any teaching that focuses more on the reward of giving than on the joy of giving. At the same time, it's completely appropriate (and biblical, I might add) to enjoy the reward that God promises and provides for those who faithfully serve Him. On this subject, it's difficult to read Scripture and come to any conclusion other than this: God loves to reward us!

We don't deserve it, but our heavenly Father delights in blessing us. Isn't that amazing?

Check out how one of the Proverbs portrays the law of the harvest: "One man gives freely, yet gains even more; another withholds unduly, but comes to poverty" (Proverbs 11:24). I love the way it's phrased in *The Message*: "The world of the generous gets larger and larger; the world of the stingy gets smaller and smaller." Some people think that by holding on to their money, they're somehow going to have more—but it doesn't work that way! I've been amazed to observe the lives of the most financially blessed people I know—the thing they all have in common is generosity.

Nowhere have I seen the truth of this proverb more clearly illustrated than in the life of my dad. If there was one thing I knew about my dad growing up, it was that he was generous! I can't begin to tell you how many times I watched with wonder as my dad would help someone out financially in their time of need or offer an encouraging word at just the right time.

Last year, my dad was diagnosed with prostate cancer. By God's grace, he's doing great today—but when people heard that he had cancer and would be having surgery, he was flooded with an outpouring of kindness that can only be described as unusual. From coast to coast, in phone calls and emails, my dad was overwhelmed by the continual stream of well wishes that he received, many of them from people he hadn't talked to in years. It was like people were coming out of the woodwork when my dad needed it most. That confirmed this powerful principle in my heart. My dad had spent a lifetime ensuring that others were well—an anonymous check here, a timely phone call there—and that generosity overflowed right back into his situation at just the right time. We really do reap what we sow!

I love Christina's story of reward … Christina's family was facing some major financial challenges—because of health issues, neither of her parents were able to work. Needless to say, the money was really tight. But that didn't stop Christina! A few weeks into the project, she came up to my wife, Casey, on a Wednesday night and asked her if she would buy a friendship bracelet. She had made the bracelets and was selling them to support her missions goal. Casey gladly bought four at $3 each. (When my wife has an opportunity to buy something that supports a great cause, she always feels the need to buy it in bulk!) Christina explained that she had raised about $50 to that point, but wanted to raise a total of $200.

We were so proud of Christina! In spite of her family's financial situation, she didn't view herself as a victim. She wasn't making excuses. Instead, she stepped out in faith and made a $200 pledge in the Realife missions drive. Later that week, we told Christina's story to my sister and brother-in-law. When my brother-in-law heard about her sacrifice, he was moved and ordered 50 right then and there (and wrote a check for $150)!

That Wednesday night in youth service, I was sharing stories of students who were stepping out in faith and working hard and how God was rewarding them in return. Christina was sitting on the front row. "Take Christina, for example." I said.

Looking at Christina, I spoke directly to her: "Things are pretty tight right now. Times are challenging, but I'm so proud of you!" She was beaming. "You are doing your part making bracelets and trusting God to do His. By the way, the Lord is honoring your efforts. I just had someone place an order for 50 of your bracelets … it looks like you just hit your goal!"

The joy in the room was electric—the students cheered. Christina cried, overwhelmed at the way God had rewarded her step of faith!

From Alicia to Christina to my dad, I love to see all of the different ways that God rewards us when we're committed to overflow. As exciting as it is to be rewarded by God for our generosity here and now, what's really incredible is the fact that our giving will also be rewarded in heaven. The reality is that most of the people who will read this book are already rich according to global standards (remember what we covered in Chapter 1). While it's wonderful to be blessed in this life, any kind of material reward is only temporary. We can't take it with us when we die.

What's really incredible is that our commitment to generosity is storing up treasures in heaven.

First Timothy 6:17-19 puts it this way: "Command those who are rich in this present world not to be arrogant nor to put their hope in wealth, which is so uncertain, but to put their hope in God, who richly provides us with everything for our enjoyment. Command them to do good, to be rich in good deeds, and to be generous and willing to share. In this way they will lay up treasure for themselves as a firm foundation for the coming age, so that they may take hold of the life that is truly life."

I can't wait for heaven! The fact that we will be rewarded in heaven for our generosity on earth is pretty amazing—but even more so is the fact that other people will be in heaven as a direct result of that giving. That's the ultimate in overflow! I don't know about you, but the fact that my gift has the potential to make an eternal difference in someone's life makes me want to give right now!

"God is able to make all grace abound to you, so that in all things at all times, having all that you need, you will abound in every good work" (2 Corinthians 9:8).

Did You Know ...

As a group, teenagers spent over $158 billion in 2005 and were predicted to have spent $205 billion in 2008!

(Adotas Advertising)

application questions

1. Why is it that sometimes we falsely expect to reap a reward when we haven't sown seeds that will produce that reward?

2. Can you think of times where "the law of the harvest" has been evident in your life (even beyond issues of money)?

3. What biblical promises can you hold onto when you don't see an immediate reward to your giving?

4. What do you imagine your reward in heaven will be like, based on your current generosity?

5. What can you do to ensure that you make an even greater impact on earth and receive an even greater reward in heaven?

you

Do you remember Scott, my old roommate? I guess you could say that he knows what it means to live an overflowing life, because the dishwasher incident that I shared at the beginning of this book was really just a warm-up for a similar experience with the washing machine.

A few months after the dishwasher situation, a group of students and leaders were over at my house for a prayer meeting. We met every week in my basement to hang out and pray. I don't remember if we were praying when it happened—perhaps we were going around the circle taking prayer requests or praise reports. Let's just say we were having a Kumbaya moment when someone noticed that a large section of the ceiling was about to cave in! Saturated by a steady stream of water that was dripping down the walls and onto the carpeted floor, the ceiling looked like its days (or hours) were numbered.

Call it common sense, or the wisdom of experience, or extraordinary spiritual discernment from some kind of prayer hangover, but two things were clear to me in that moment: first, the water was coming from the washing machine (which was located precisely above the saggy spot in the ceiling); and second, my roommate was most likely involved.

The washing machine had been disconnected because I was having tile work done in the laundry room. Scott needed to do a load of laundry, so he reconnected the washer and went to town. Let me just take a moment to note that I was impressed that he used the correct detergent this time! It would've been a real bummer if my basement was flooded with—I don't know—liquid bubbles (been there, done that) ... or tub and tile cleaner ... or transmission fluid. We were making progress, after all! The problem this time was that Scott hadn't put the water hose on tight enough when he reconnected it. The resulting deluge put our prayer meeting on pause and made me think long and hard about getting flood insurance to cover any more potential damages from my roommate.

Are You Ready?

Are you ready to live an overflowing life? Are you ready to be used by God in such a powerful way that the people around you are swept up in God, refreshed and renewed? If so, then there are three key truths about overflow that I'd encourage you to consider and embrace as you start your own journey in generosity. You've seen them illustrated in the student stories throughout this book.

Imagine what God will do if you apply them in your own life.

1. You are an empty container.

The first thing you have to understand about overflow is that your life is an empty container—nothing more and nothing less. Unfortunately, a lot of people miss out on what God would do because they go to one extreme or another.

On the one hand, there are those who think that they're God's gift to humanity. This kind of person overestimates how important they are in the big picture. They wonder how God would make it without their help, forgetting or ignoring the fact that God created the universe and everything in it out of nothing. They forget that God knows everything, He's everywhere present, and He has the power to do whatever He wants. He's God and He doesn't need our help! Anything that we're able to contribute is only possible because He wills and enables it. Without Him, we are nothing.

On the other hand, there are those who don't see how valuable they really are. They underestimate their role in the big scheme of things, failing to understand how much their life matters to God and to His Kingdom. They wonder how God could work in or through them. Or they don't see how they could possibly give enough to make a difference. Maybe you can relate. If so, you need to understand that your life is incredibly valuable—priceless, in fact. And regardless of the amount you can give, you were created in God's image with a divine purpose to fulfill.

The little you can give is much when God is in it. He doesn't need you, but He created you anyway. Imagine that! He loves you and has a plan for your life.

If you're going to live a life that overflows, you've got to keep the right perspective. God doesn't need us. In fact, Jesus said that apart from Him we can't do anything (John 15:5). Our lives are completely empty and meaningless apart from Him. And yet, He's chosen to include us. God wants to work through us. For that reason, each of us is incredibly important.

So, what does it mean to be a container? We were created to hold something. God created us to carry His life, light, and love to a dying world. God wants to fill our life in such a rich way that it spills out and blesses others. Whether or not we allow Him to do that, though, is up to us—which brings us to the second principle of overflow.

2. God is an abundant source.

Everything in the container that is your life comes from a source. For example, when you fill a glass of water in the sink, the faucet is your source.

There are good sources and there are bad sources. At some point, we've all filled up at a bad source. We've all taken shortcuts in our attempt to experience the satisfaction of an overflowing life. You can probably think of a time in your life when you tried to fill your container with junk—stuff that didn't satisfy. But then you came to God. He saved you, turned your life upside down, and shook all of the junk out. God knew that you weren't created to carry that stuff. If He hadn't done something, it would've destroyed your life. Aren't you glad He saved you?

Now that you're a follower of Christ, you understand that what you put in your container matters. Where you go to fill your life makes all the difference. When you put Jesus in charge of your life, your container will be filled full to overflowing with everything good. When you offer God the empty container of your life, He will fill it up. And you'll experience the greatest love, the greatest joy, and the greatest peace. What's really exciting is that everyone around you will be impacted as a result.

The cool thing about God is that He is infinite in every way. He cannot be limited in any way. His resources are unending.

When you go to God with your life, you're going to an abundant source. He doesn't just know what you need, He's able to provide it. The Bible says that God is able to do "exceeding abundantly beyond all that we ask or imagine" (Ephesians 3:20, paraphrased).

You could spend your entire life searching for a source to fill your container, something other than God that will satisfy. You won't find one. You will never find anything that could even compare to God, let alone match Him. Your best friends will disappoint you. There are things money can't buy. And the pleasures this world has to offer are short-lived at best. Not only is God able to satisfy your deepest desires and longings, He is able to work through you to do great things. God wants you to dream big dreams and do big things for His glory! He wants you to overflow. As you'll see in the next section, you can, with His help.

3. You can give out without running out—overflow.

The reason God wants to fill your life with His goodness isn't just for your enjoyment. Sure, He wants to fill you full up, but He also wants to overflow through you! The cool thing about the way that works, is that with God's help, you can give out without running out. You'd think that by giving, we would end up with less, but that's not how it works in God's economy! Remember the Proverb we read last chapter: "The world of the generous gets larger and larger; the world of the stingy gets smaller and smaller" (Proverbs 11:24, *The Message*).

On any given day, you're surrounded by opportunities to overflow.

And remember, overflow works in every area of your life—it's not just about money. There's that kid in class, the one with the tough situation at home. He could use your encouragement and friendship. There's the attendant at the gas station where you fill up every week. She needs to know about God's love. There's that family member who knows the truth of God's Word, but has yet to accept it. They need your consistent example. When you're connected to God, His life can overflow through you in all of these situations and more—you can give out without running out.

As exciting as an overflowing life is, sometimes we are tempted to give up. We get discouraged because we don't see the impact we are making right away. But the Bible teaches us to push on: "Let us not become weary in doing good, for at the proper time we will reap a harvest *if we do not give up*" (Galatians 6:9, emphasis mine). Remember, if you plant a seed, you'll harvest a crop. If you make an investment in someone for God, you're going to get a return on that investment. We plant the seed and water, but God is the one who makes it grow in its time (1 Corinthians 3:7-8). We can trust God with the results!

Dream a Big Dream and Do a Big Thing

Are you ready to dream a big dream and do a big thing for God? Are you ready for God to overflow in your life—just like He did in the lives of the students and leaders of Realife. I know God is ready. Just imagine all of the different ways God could overflow in your life to make a difference in someone else's. The effects could literally be felt around the world! If that's going to happen, you've got to recognize that you can't do it on your own. If that's going to happen, you've got to stay connected to God. If that's going to happen, you've got to be willing to give of yourself. When you do, you'll experience overflow, the most exciting and satisfying life you could ever live!

As I write the final sentences of this book, I've paused a little bit to think back through the amazing stories of overflow that you've just read. I've stopped to think about you—and the countless students just like you who are going to be inspired and equipped by these stories. I remind myself of the enormous need out there—and I start to wonder ...

I wonder how many missionaries are going to get the supplies they need because, from this day forward, you choose to give generously and sacrificially. I wonder how many missionaries will stay on the mission field, not needing to return home for grueling fund-raising trips, because you're willing to go without that daily latte or that next CD. I wonder how many hungry people will be fed. I wonder how many who have never tasted clean water will get their first glass. I wonder how many children will be rescued from the horrific sex trade.

I wonder how many people will be in heaven instead of hell ... because of your generosity.

God only knows! And the only way you're going to know, is if you let Him overflow through you. With God's help, let's dream a big dream and do a big thing!

Did You Know ...

For just $1 per day, you can sponsor a child in one of the world's poorest countries—providing them with nutritious food, medical care, education, social development, and a safe environment.

application questions

1. Are there any items in the "container" of your life that would prevent you from living a life of overflow?

2. How do you plan on getting rid of those things? How will you keep them from becoming a part of your life again?

3. What are some opportunities that you can take advantage of now to overflow, either through your giving or otherwise?

4. After reading this book, what is the dream that God has placed on your heart? How does God want to overflow through your life to help others?

5. Who are some people that God has placed in your life right now that can be an encouragement to you as you fulfill that dream? Who are the people in your life that need your encouragement to experience overflow?

overflow ideas

There are so many ways you can experience overflow. Here are a handful of practical ideas to get you started:

+ Ashley drew sketches of students at Realife for a donation—and raised over $100!

+ One of our small groups got sponsors for free throws and raised several hundred dollars by making baskets for Jesus.

+ One student at Realife bought candy in bulk and sold it for a profit. Sweet!

+ Many students collected their own loose change as well as change from their family or anyone else willing to donate.

+ In case you'd like to know … my two oldest daughters sold snow cones at our summer camp and raised $407 for missions! Thanks for caring!

about the author

Scotty Gibbons has been the director of Realife Student Ministries at James River Assembly since 1993. When he started, Scotty could drive the entire youth group around in a van. Today, the Realife Student Center is home to more than 1,000 students and 200 volunteer leaders.

He has authored two other books: *Carry-On* and *First Things First*.

Scotty is a nationally recognized youth communicator with a passion for reaching students and equipping leaders. Scotty, his wife, Casey, and their daughters live in Ozark, Missouri.

want to grow in God?

volume 1

first things first

scotty gibbons

a devotional for students

order online!
scottygibbons.com

What's the first thing you do after your alarm clock sounds? After you hit "snooze" fifteen times?

How you start your morning impacts the rest of your day. That's why this book is so important. It's a practical resource that will help you put *First Things First*.

· Helps students establish a daily time with God
· Makes growing in your understanding of Scripture and prayer fun
· Perfect for students with busy lives

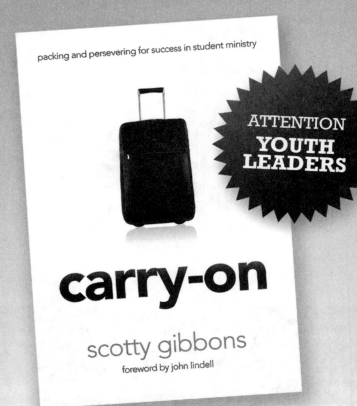

for more information about
Onward Books:

onwardbooks.com

---

for *Overflow* bulk orders:

overflowexperience.com